Spiritual Protection in One Minute

J. Kirk Johnston

Dedication

This book is dedicated to my parents,
Wendell and Martha,
who were the first to teach me
about spiritual warfare.
Thanks for steering me in the
right direction!

Acknowledgements

Gayle Johnston — for typing up endless revisions, and, in general, loving me through this process.

Kim Richardson — for putting in an unbelievable number of hours editing this manuscript.

Chris Gould — for believing in this book and helping to make it a reality.

Andrew Hasebroock — for quickly and professionally illustrating this book.

Aaron Bullian — for helping make this book happen and encouraging me to do it.

Table of Contents

Introduction

There are certain days throughout history that will be remembered in vivid detail. Talk to someone old enough to have been alive on December 7, 1941, and that person invariably recalls exactly where he or she was, and precisely what was happening the moment the news was heard that Pearl Harbor had been bombed. It is truly "a day that will live in infamy." The same is true for November 22, 1963. I was in second grade in Ft. Worth, Texas on that tragic day when President Kennedy was assassinated. I can still see clearly in my mind's eye my teacher rushing out of our classroom and then returning in tears. While it was difficult for her to speak, I can hear her telling us that the president had been shot. I remember, like it was yesterday, looking around the room at the stunned faces of my classmates. It is a day I will never forget, and it changed the way I look at life.

Likewise, Americans know exactly where they were and what they were doing when they heard the news that two planes had been flown into the World

Trade Center. That day changed the way we look at the world; it was no longer a safe place. We all realized we are in grave danger. We were shocked by the realization that there are people in this world who hate us enough to try to kill us by any means possible. We woke up to the fact that, on any given day, at any moment, we could be attacked again by an enemy committed to our destruction. Not that we were completely oblivious to the reality of evil people before 9/11, nor is it true that security measures were non-existent before that day, but, September 11, 2001, forced us to accept the fact that there was and is a war going on. We are under siege, so we must protect our loved ones and ourselves with greater priority and urgency. That message was painfully driven home for us on that terrible day, and I believe there is a parallel in the spiritual realm.

In Ephesians 6:13, we read about what Paul calls "the evil day." This is what I believe is the spiritual equivalent to the day the Twin Towers fell. Tony Evans describes it this way, "That's the day when your number comes up, so to speak...when Satan is going to unleash the forces of hell on you."[1] The point is that for every Christian there is an "evil day" when Satan is going to attack viciously and without warning.

Some of you reading this know exactly what I am talking about. You have already experienced an evil day. Before it happened, you might have believed there was a malevolent entity called Satan, and you probably assumed that he was up to no good, but it wasn't until your spiritual 9/11 that you fully realized how much danger you were in and how much damage Satan could inflict. It never fully hit you that there was a spiritual war going on, but now you know!

Perhaps you are reading this, and you have never experienced a spiritual 9/11. You are aware of the existence of Satan and his demons, and you realize that he is strongly opposed to God and his people, but, up to this point in your life as a Christian, Satan has not been an urgent issue for you. He hasn't seriously affected either you or your loved ones. The truth is the evil day is coming, and you need to be ready for it.

The reality for those who have already experienced Satan's attacks is that it could happen again. The evil day is not just a one-time occurrence. It can happen again and again, and it can happen any day, without any warning.

In I Peter 5:8, Peter tells us that, "...the devil prowls around like a roaring lion, seeking someone to devour." This word "devour" can literally refer to consuming something, but used in a spiritual and figurative sense, it refers to ruin or destruction. I believe that Satan desires to ruin the life of every Christian, especially those trying to live for Jesus. Since Satan can't rob us of our salvation, he wants to destroy our lives while we are here on earth. He will try to undermine your testimony for Christ and render you ineffective for God. He will fight to destroy your family and relationships. He will attempt to take away your God-given peace, joy, and contentment. In short, he has declared all-out war against you! This is why every day we need to be properly prepared for whatever Satan may throw at us.

This book is designed to help you clearly understand that God, through His Word and by the Spirit, has enabled you to hold your ground against Satan. It is possible to prepare for spiritual battle with a little understanding and practice. I urge you along with the apostle Paul to "take up the full armor of God"! It can be done – I assure you. You can achieve *Spiritual Protection in One Minute*.

Chapter 1

Our Authority in Christ

During the Civil War after a string of defeats at the hands of the Confederate Army, President Abraham Lincoln picked a handsome, young officer named George McClellan to be commander of the Union Army. After he received word of his promotion, McClellan wrote his wife, "I don't feel any different than I did yesterday. Indeed, I have not yet put on my new uniform. I am sure that I am in command of the Union Army, however, because President Lincoln's order to that effect now lies before me."[2]

This personal note from a Civil War general is a reminder of a very important foundational issue. When we trust Christ as Savior, at that moment, we become soldiers in the Lord's army,[3] and we are given the authority to defend ourselves against Satan. You may not see yourself as a soldier or feel any different, but you are in Christ. Before you put on the first piece of spiritual armor, you must understand what your authority is in Christ, and that with it, you have the spiritual power to do battle with Satan.

Paul says, "I pray that the eyes of your heart may be enlightened, so that you may know what is the hope of His calling, what are the riches of the glory of His inheritance in the saints, and what is the surpassing power toward us who believe."[4] At some point God has to open our spiritual eyes to see that all the power we need to wage war against the powers of darkness is available to us in Christ. That power comes from the fact that Christ is seated at the right hand of God in heaven,[5] where He has been given authority over all things.[6] A most wonderful truth is that God "...has raised us up with Him, and seated us with Him...."[7] What the Bible is saying is that we as Christian soldiers share in the authority, and thus the power of the risen Christ! When we recognize that we have been given the authority and power of our commander-in-chief, Jesus Christ, to do battle with Satan, we are properly plugged into our power source, and we can carry out whatever orders our commander gives us. This is what Paul is referring to when he says, "Be strong in the Lord, and in the strength of His might."[8] This, by the way, is a very important point. Our authority and power in Christ is only effective for the orders given to us by Christ, and when we exceed our orders, we may experience severe consequences.

You may be aware of the terrible incident in Iraq where American soldiers exceeded their orders at Abu Ghraib prison. Some of the soldiers humiliated and tortured Iraqi prisoners of war. After extensive investigation, it was discovered that certain men and women were abusing their authority, and the power given to them through their commanders. While this unfortunate incident gave the U.S. military a black eye, it also led to the court martial of the guilty soldiers. What a tragic situation! It can happen in the spiritual realm as well.

When we exceed our spiritual orders and do things in the name of Christ that He has not commanded us to do, there can be serious consequences for us too. We must be very sure about what our commander-in-chief has given us the authority to do.

For instance, we have not been ordered to exercise demons. I realize that many Christian leaders say this is one of the most important things for us to do in spiritual warfare.[9] It is also true that Christ gave orders to seventy of His disciples at one point to cast out demons,[10] but it is very important to note that by the time the apostle Paul was ministering, casting out demons was no longer the order of the day.

In one account, we find Paul ministering in Philippi while being followed and repeatedly called out by a slave girl in-dwelt by a demon.[11] This slave girl hounded Paul for "many days." If Christians at that time were under orders to exorcise demons, Paul should have done so at first contact with the girl. Instead, he apparently tried to ignore her. Finally, in frustration, days later, he cast out the demon. The lesson from this is that the apostle Paul did not view exorcism as a command from the Lord to be immediately carried out. Rather it was something to be done only if deemed necessary under the circumstances. The truth is we are not given orders in the New Testament epistles to cast out demons. It may at times be something we believe the Lord wants us to do, but we should be very careful about doing so because it is not included in our latest written orders from the commander.

In addition, we have not been given orders to "bind Satan." Again, I recognize that this is widely encouraged by many Christian leaders and spiritual warfare experts.[12] The rationale comes from this: "How can anyone enter the strong man's house and carry off his property, unless he first binds the strong man? And then he will plunder his house."[13] The truth is that Christ has already triumphed over the enemy. He has already disarmed and humiliated them.[14] Our responsibility is to hold the ground He has already taken. The reality is that Matthew 16:19 is not commanding us to bind Satan. That verse is, first of all, not addressing the binding of. "whomever," but "whatever." It's not about persons; instead it's about practices. Beyond that, it is saying that whatever is bound by church leaders on earth has already been bound in heaven. Church leaders are only to announce what God has already decided to do, not initiate new policies.

Bottom line, can we ask God to restrain or bind Satan when we are proclaiming the Gospel or doing something else He has ordered us to do? Yes, and perhaps Christ will answer that prayer affirmatively, but it also may be that He wants us to stand up to Satan and grow in our faith in the process. Whatever

God ultimately decided to do in regard to "binding Satan," that is His prerogative, not ours.

This is true in one more area as well—rebuking Satan. It's not unusual to turn on the television and see some evangelist or pastor rebuking Satan. This is standard operating procedure in some Christian circles. However, when Michael the archangel got into an argument with Satan over the body of Moses, he did not rebuke Satan, rather he said, "The Lord rebuke you."[15] In Jude 9, it is clear that a "rebuke" is pronouncing judgment on another. When a person tells Satan to "go back to the pit" or consigns him to hell, that is pronouncing judgment. Obviously, Michael did not understand rebuking Satan to be an order for us from the throne. Rather, he saw it as something to come directly from the throne.

Exorcising demons and binding and rebuking Satan are just a few of the things Christ has not ordered us to do. Interestingly enough, these are all offensive maneuvers, and we have not been ordered to go on the offensive against Satan. Rather, we have one main, standing order[16] "...Resist the devil, and he will flee from you."

The word *resist* is a military term. It was often used in ancient times to refer to military sentries who were given an important post to guard. It was their job to guard that post and make sure the enemy did not infiltrate that position. This is the assignment that we as Christian soldiers have been given. All of us have been assigned a spiritual post. That spiritual turf certainly includes our own lives, but it may also involve protecting those in our church, school or family from Satan as well. The point is we have been called to defend what Christ has already won.

As Tony Evans put it, "Jesus has already invaded Satan's domain and won back all the territory Adam lost...so our job is to hold the ground Jesus has won...remember that we are fighting from victory, not for victory."[17]

Ours is a defensive war, and this is further underscored by Paul telling us three times to "stand firm."[18] This is yet another military term. It was used in reference to holding on to critical military positions. Whatever spiritual post God has given us to defend, it is very important; and we need to hold onto it for our benefit and God's glory. However, it is not going to be easy: "...our struggle is not against flesh and blood, but against the rulers, against the powers, against the world forces of this darkness, against the spiritual forces of wickedness in the heavenly places."[19]

This verse tells us, first of all, that the war we are in with Satan is a "struggle." This word may not sound that serious, but it is. It refers to desperate hand-to-hand combat when the fighting is vicious and to the death, and it also was used to refer to wrestling matches where there were no rules and no holds' barred. In other words, we are in a war with Satan where he is not going to play fair. He will do anything to defeat you, and it is either going to be him or you.

This portion of Scripture also indicates that Satan has a vast army lined up against us. The terms "rulers," "powers," "world forces," and "spiritual forces" are all ranks of demons. Like any effective army, there has to be a chain of command with different ranks of officers and soldiers. Satan has organized his demons into different classifications and each has specific orders.[20] Some demon, at some point, will have orders to attack you, and that is why you need to be protected and aware of his tactics.

One of Satan's favorite schemes is to try to convince believers in Jesus Christ that he still has authority over them. Fred Dickason speaks in one of his books about a time when he was conversing with a demon who called himself "Throne"[21] – that is almost certainly his military rank. This, by the way, is one of those practices we do not have orders to do and, therefore, is not recommended. Nevertheless, in this conversation "Throne" revealed to the counselor that in actuality he has no authority over believers whatsoever, but his objective was clearly to convince uninformed Christians that he does.

This is one of Satan's most frequently used strategies. If he can lie and deceive us into thinking that he still has power over us, then effectively he does, and we are going to be spiritually defeated. This is why Christians must accept the written word of our commander-in-chief that we are seated with Him, spiritually speaking, at the right hand of the Father. We share His power and authority in the war against Satan. There is no reason why we should be defeated, but, unfortunately, many Christians are.

Billy Graham once publicly stated that he believes most Christians are leading spiritually defeated lives. This is shocking, but as a pastor for over twenty-five years, I know many Christians are regularly losing their battles with Satan. To a great extent, this is true because believers do not realize their spiritual authority in Christ. H owever, another significant reason is that many believers fail to "put on the full armor of God" each day.

There's more to spiritual protection than simply understanding what the full armor of God is. Knowing how to put it on is just as important. What purpose does the knowledge serve if we don't act on it? It would be comparable to a football player, knowing full well that he has protective gear, yet choosing to go on the field to face his opponents without it. He makes himself vulnerable with every piece of gear left behind. The same holds true for us in the spiritual realm. We must put on the full armor of God to fully protect ourselves. I assure you, it is quick and easy to do. We start with the belt of truth.

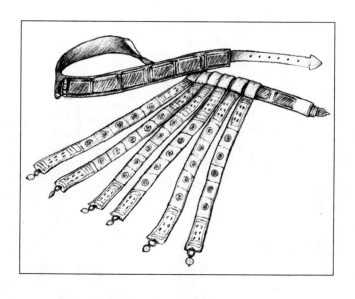

The Belt of Truth

Chapter 2

The Belt of Truth

Three years after the terrorist attack on September 11, 2001, the director of the CIA called a press conference. He was apparently concerned that Americans were becoming complacent or less vigilant about terrorism because there had not been any further attacks in the U.S. He warned that new terrorist attacks could come, but they might be perpetrated in a different form; he suggested that the next assaults could be chemical or biological. This has caused me to do some personal research about these new forms of weaponry and how we should protect ourselves in case of an attack. Although far from an expert, I discovered that the only way to live through this type of attack is to prevent contact with the chemical/biological agent.

Exposure to even small amounts of a dangerous chemical can do serious damage. As an example, one milligram of Sarin, a nerve agent, inhaled in the lungs is lethal. Likewise, one milligram of VX (even more caustic) on any exposed skin will kill, too. In the case of a chemical warfare attack, protective clothing must be non-porous and leak-free, and it must cover the entire body. Remember, even limited exposure will cause death; therefore, to survive a chemical fallout, full, protective gear must be worn at all times, or at the every least, it must be easily and quickly donned to be effective.

How do these principles apply in our spiritual life? In Ephesians 6:11, Paul tells us to "put on the full armor of God." Right after this command, Paul says something very similar in verse 13, "Take up the full armor of God." In both of these verses extreme urgency is expressed; there is no time to waste. The verb "take up" is a military term speaking of final battle preparations. The point is that we need to be wearing the armor of God all the time. We should not wait for an attack by Satan to guard ourselves, but if we are caught without our armor, we need to be able to put it on quickly, and completely, so that we are fully protected.

It is significant that Paul in these two verses tells us to put on the *full* armor of God. Nothing is more toxic to our spiritual lives than Satan's lies and accusations, and it doesn't take much to do incredible damage. We can't expect to do battle with Satan and win if we are only wearing part of God's protective armor. This is why so many Christians today are spiritually demoralized: they have allowed themselves to be vulnerable because they are not wearing the armor, they don't know how to put it on quickly, or they are only wearing part of it. What prevents us as Christians from wearing the full armor when God, in His perfection, provided us this impenetrable uniform? Most likely it is because we do not clearly understand the individual pieces of the protective gear and how each piece is put in place. Unlike gas masks and protective suits, "...the weapons of our warfare are not of the flesh...."[22] Our weapons are spiritual, not physical. This can lead to a lot of confusion. This is why Paul compares the pieces of spiritual armor with the uniform of a Roman soldier. While this was a useful demonstration then, we don't live in Roman times, so many of us are not familiar with their battle attire. Some of us have a mental picture of what the Roman armor looks like, but unfortunately that picture is probably the dress uniform of the soldier. Paul most likely didn't have in mind the dress uniform but the armor used in actual combat. These are very different outfits: one was meant for show the other was meant for battle. The combat armor is what the Legionnaires put on to go out and fight the enemy. With this in mind, let's take a closer look at the different pieces of spiritual armor, beginning with the Belt of Truth.

When Paul talks about "...having girded your loins with truth,"[23] he is referring to one of three possible different belts worn by Romans soldiers. I believe this particular belt was the one that was worn into combat. It was a thick leather belt with leather strips that hung down over the lower part of the soldier's torso. This belt had three purposes: the belt provided a stable place to hang weapons such as a sword; the belt held the tunic tightly in place and gave complete freedom of movement; and the belt afforded the soldier some protection for his abdomen and lower torso. How can we relate this belt to our spiritual protection?

In ancient times the bowels were considered to be the seat of all deep feelings. This is probably the origin of what we sometimes refer to today as a "gut feeling." People believed that the deepest emotions of anger, compassion, bitterness and love came from the "gut." So when Paul talks about the belt of truth and putting it around our waist, he is indicating that truth is what should protect and inform our deepest feelings, not vice versa. The belt of truth represents our commitment to hold onto that place which harnesses our feelings, keeping them in check and informing our emotions of what is really true.

The importance of this is seen in Adam and Eve's first encounter with Satan in the Garden of Eden. In the Genesis 3 account of the fall of mankind into sin, "feelings" played a very important role in enticing them to sin. You may remember that Satan began his initial approach to Eve with a very emotionally charged statement that accused God of being unfair to them. He said, "Indeed, has God said, 'you shall not eat of any tree of the garden.'"[24] Satan deliberately misrepresented what God said earlier in order to see if he could provoke an emotional response from Eve, and he was testing her knowledge by adding and subtracting from what God really said. When Eve responded by supplementing and deleting what God had said,[25] Satan knew she was vulnerable and moved in for the kill, spiritually speaking. He directly contradicted what God said about certain death if one ate the forbidden fruit, and he made another accusation against God's goodness.[26] This was to encourage Eve to swell with feelings of pride. It worked. Her fragile commitment to truth completely dissipated, and she let her emotions run freely. She saw it was good food, which looked wonderful, and that she would be much wiser after eating it, so she gave in to her feelings and ate. Adam was nearby. He realized that Eve, his partner and only other human, was doomed. He ate knowing what he was doing was wrong, but he wanted to be with the woman he loved, no matter the consequence. He ate what was given to him. The result was that Satan claimed a major spiritual victory over both of them with terrible and lasting consequences for all of us. Simply stated, Adam and Eve let their feelings overcome their commitment to the truth.

The first piece of spiritual armor that we need to put on is the belt of truth. This is *a commitment to believing what God says is true rather than giving in to our emotions and desires*. It is first knowing what God says is true and then making the decision to believe that truth, no matter how we feel at a particular moment.

Now this is not to imply that feelings are bad. Part of the image of God in us is our emotions, and they are an important and wonderful aspect of who we are. God has created us with emotions, in part, to indicate to us what we are thinking or believing at any particular time. When we begin to feel something strongly, we should not immediately act on those feelings, but rather, we should ask ourselves what is the source of those emotions. If the source is erroneous thoughts or beliefs, then we should correct those thoughts and beliefs to bring them in line with God's truth. This means that we have to be more committed to what God has said is true, than what we may feel at the moment. This was certainly true for Adam and Eve back in the garden, but it is even more challenging for us today because we have an additional problem they didn't have –the "flesh."

Now, our actual flesh powerfully urges us to eat, for instance, because our bodies truly need nutrition. Just like Eve, we see beautiful food and our human flesh tells us we need it. We do need food, but as Paul teaches, we should not let it control us.[27] God does not want us to be gluttons; therefore, we should meet our legitimate human needs, like nourishment, in a way that honors God and is best for our bodies. However, Satan is going to regularly tempt us to address our needs in a way that dishonors God and causes harm to us personally, and he will consistently team up with our immaterial flesh to urge us to meet needs that are illegitimate.

The "flesh" is an immaterial aspect of every person, including believers in Jesus Christ. Paul talks extensively about his struggle with the flesh in Romans 7:15-25. His repeated use of present tense verbs makes it difficult to accept that this passage is speaking only of his life B.C., that is, Before Christ. Rather, it is clear that this was an ongoing battle for Paul, as it is for every believer. Every one of us regularly experiences strong urges or cravings that feel like real needs. However, if these feelings of need come from the "flesh," they are illegitimate. James talked about these illegitimate desires and said they are the source of internal conflict as well as actual fights among Christian brothers and sisters.[28]

Several years ago, a man came to see me with a terrible problem. Every day when he finished his work at the office, he felt an incredible urge to view pornography. Almost daily he would go down the street and rent an "adult" video, watch it back at his office, and then return home late for dinner. After a couple of years of this, his wife, understandably, was beside herself, and extremely bitter towards him. His relationship with her was in ruin. He was a very young Christian and did not know what to do. He figured that because he felt the desire for pornography so strongly, he must really need it. His rationalization was an attempt to hide his true fear: if it was wrong, how could he possibly overcome such powerful feelings? I explained to him that no one *needs* to look at pornography. We have legitimate physical needs that, for God's glory and our ultimate well being, should be met in a committed, loving relationship. Even though Satan tries to make us see it differently, the craving for pornography is an illegitimate need. When Satan tempts us to indulge our desires; he tells us that they are real and must be addressed immediately, by any possible means. It's important to clarify that Satan is not the source of our illegitimate desires;[29] rather it is our immaterial flesh. When our flesh begins to make us feel we need something, Satan chimes in and tells us, "Oh yes, you do need _____" (whatever it is), when, in fact, we don't. He works in concert with our immaterial flesh and our actual flesh to urge us to do things that will dishonor our Lord and destroy our lives. He will encourage us to follow our feelings or as many put it today, our "heart." Instead, we should put on the first piece of our spiritual armor each day: the belt of truth. We do this by making the commitment (and I believe it should be made out loud): "Lord, today I am going to believe whatever You say is true and is best for me, regardless of how I feel any given moment." When we make this commitment sincerely, we are on our way to spiritual victory.

Now someone might say that if we "walk by the Spirit . . . [we] will not carry out the desire of the flesh."[30] That's very true, but what does it mean to "walk by the Spirit?" It means that as the Spirit reminds us of God's truth as we go through our day, we can choose to listen to Him, or we can listen to our "feelings" and Satan's urging to act on them. Our commitment to put on the belt of truth is critical. We need to make that decision before we are confronted by temptation. However, putting on just one piece of our spiritual armor will not be enough – it still leaves us susceptible. Complete protection also requires the second piece of armor – the breastplate of righteousness.

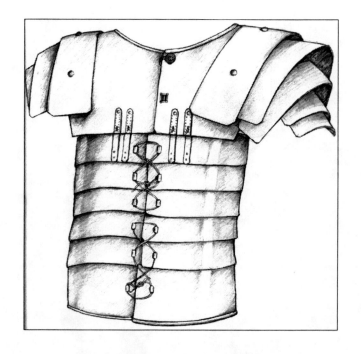

The Breastplate of Righteousness

Chapter 3

The Breastplate of Righteousness

I had no real idea what I was getting into years ago when I agreed to counsel with a woman, who called me out of the blue, asking for help. She did not attend the church where I was the senior pastor, and I had never met the woman. In fact, I didn't know anything about her. With that said, I sensed the Lord telling me to meet with her anyway.

On the agreed-upon day she showed up at my office with a close girlfriend and began to pour out her story. It was incredible! She told me that she had a problem with shoplifting. At the oddest times and in the craziest ways, she would steal items from stores that didn't make any sense for her to take. Food, practical clothing, and other necessities were not on her shoplifting list; she generally didn't even care about the inventory of items she had just taken. She felt compelled to steal the items. The reasons were immaterial. Yes, she definitely had a problem, and she knew it.

She spent literally two hundred thousand dollars beyond the limits of her insurance seeking counseling and therapy to combat her urges to pilfer. She took just about every kind of pill to treat a variety of disorders. Even though she had invested an enormous amount of time and money seeking a cure for her "illness," she was still stealing things she didn't really want and taking things she didn't really need. To add insult to injury, she had just recently been caught, again. The authorities were no longer amused by her little "habit" and were threatening to lock her up and throw away the key. Her husband had given her an ultimatum: either stop stealing now or divorce papers were on the way. She was desperate and out of both money and options. She didn't know me, but someone told her I might be able to help. I wasn't so sure I could help her, but I was certain that I could identify her problem: she was losing spiritual battles because she wasn't putting on the full armor of God.

In Ephesians 6:14, God commands us to "stand firm, therefore, having girded your loins with truth, and having put on the breastplate of righteousness." Because both of these phrases use the word "having," the English translation might lead us to believe that the action is something we do once, and never need to do again.

It is true that when we trusted Christ as Savior we were clothed with Him and His righteousness,[31] and that now God sees us as righteous in Christ. However, what Paul is pointing out is that in order to stand firm against Satan's attacks we have to regularly and habitually put on what he calls the "breastplate of righteousness."

For many people, this term conjures up the picture of a Roman soldier with a huge single plate of metal strapped to his chest. This mental picture is not completely accurate. In battle, the Legionnaires wore a piece of armor with overlapping plates of metal that covered all the torso including the shoulders and back, right down to the waist. It was extremely difficult for the enemy to penetrate the breastplate with any weapon, and its design allowed complete freedom of movement. When the Roman soldier was wearing the *segmentata* into battle, he could be supremely confident that his vital organs were protected against injury.

Spiritually speaking, we put on the breastplate of righteousness whenever we consciously acknowledge that we are "saints" because of our belief in Christ.[32] This does not mean that we are sinless in our daily lives. We all sin every day in a number of ways and to deny this is self-deception.[33] With that said, it is very important that we see ourselves, not as simply "sinners saved by grace" who can't help sinning whenever we are tempted by Satan; rather, we need to view ourselves as saints who can say no to any temptation with God's help. The more we see ourselves as saints, the better equipped we will be to stand firm against Satan's seductive and powerful words.

As saints, we do not have to sin. We do sin because we choose to do so. We cannot claim "the devil made me do it" because Satan cannot force us to do what is wrong. First John 5:18 indicates that believers don't have to sin; "the evil one" cannot "touch" us. The word "touch" here means a lot more than simply putting a finger on someone. It actually refers to forcibly laying hold of someone or something.[34] In the immediate context, John is saying that Satan cannot force us to sin. Satan tries to deceive us into believing that we are just weak sinners who do not have the power to say no; so when he tempts us, we will meekly give in. This is exactly what a lot of Christians today believe, including the woman who came to see me. She thought she had no control over the temptation to steal. The scriptures tell us that "…greater is He who is in you than he who is in the world."[35] This verse assures us as believers that the indwelling Holy Spirit is greater than any person **or** spirit in the world. We have the power within us to say "no" to what is wrong and say "yes" to what is right.

After finishing her sad story, I asked this lady if she was a Christian. She quickly said she was, but then she cast her eyes down. I asked her if she had just heard a voice in her head telling her she was not a "real" Christian. Startled, she said, "How did you know that?" I told her I simply know how Satan operates. I inquired about whether she was trusting in Christ alone for forgiveness of sins; she nodded affirmatively. I assured her, on that basis, she was indeed saved. However, the problem of shoplifting still needed to be addressed. I asked if she ever heard internal voices urging her to steal things. She said yes and admitted that she had never told this to anyone, including her best friend present in the room, because she was afraid of being diagnosed as "nuts." I explained that she was not insane but a victim of Satan's deception. The solution was for her to see herself as God sees her, a saint who doesn't have to listen to Satan or do what he says. She told me that in all the counseling and therapy she received, most of it from Christians, no one ever discussed the issue of spiritual warfare with her. What a tragedy! After instructions about putting on the armor of God, I sent her home with a directive to call me if she continued to steal. I never heard back from her.

Every day, we need to put on the breastplate of righteousness by verbally affirming "I am a saint who is righteous in Jesus Christ. I don't have to sin, and Satan cannot make me sin." Whenever we are tempted to sin, we must put this piece of the armor on quickly. However it is best to just have it on all the time.

I understand from my friends who served in the Vietnam War that most soldiers who were supplied with protective jackets or vests did not like to wear them. They were so bulky and it was so hot, that most times the soldiers went without this extra protection. In Iraq, this is not the case at all. It doesn't matter how hot the weather is or how uncomfortable the equipment, our soldiers in Iraq want all the protection they can get. They even buy their own protective jackets and vests if they are not issued one or if what they are issued is not sufficient to shield them. They recognize that any time they are out on patrol, even in an armored vehicle, they are vulnerable to bombs and explosive devices hidden by enemy insurgents.

The reality for us is that Satan regularly sets traps and plants bombs of temptation designed to destroy our lives. We need to put on the breastplate of righteousness every day so that we don't become a casualty in the spiritual war going on all around us. However, once again, two pieces of spiritual armor is still not enough. It is necessary that we also wear "sandals of peace."

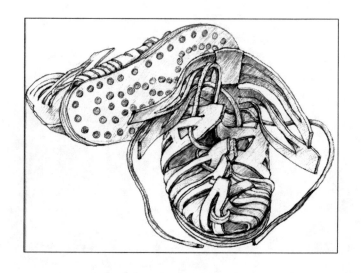

The Sandals of Peace

Chapter 4

The Sandals of Peace

Ernest Hemmingway tells a story about an incident in Spain many years ago.[36] It seems this father had a falling out with his son over something the son had done, and the young man had run away from home. The father at a certain point cooled off and decided the separation was not worth the offense. So the dad put the following in the personal section of a major newspaper in Madrid. "Paco, meet me at the hotel Montana, noon, Tuesday. All is forgiven, Papa." At the appointed time the father arrived only to find eight hundred "Pacos" seeking reconciliation.

The truth is that a lot of people, including many Christians, struggle with guilt and a need for forgiveness. Many of us find ourselves at odds with someone that we love deep down, and we would like to be at peace with him or her again. This is particularly true in our relationship with God. If we are honest with ourselves, we know that we regularly do things that are wrong in the eyes of a holy God,[37] and that we need God's forgiveness. Some Christians are strongly convinced that they are forgiven no matter what they do because of their trust in the sufficiency of Christ's death and resurrection.[38] These people have real calm and inner peace. Although, there's a significant number of believers who wrestle with the issues of guilt, forgiveness and peace with God, including people who should know better. I have known many pastors, missionaries, seminarians, and "mature" Christians who continue to struggle with these issues. One in particular comes to mind.

This man had been a pastor for many years. He was a graduate of a well-known college where he majored in Bible. He knew the Scriptures very well, perhaps better than I did, but when he came to talk with me as a fellow pastor and friend, he was in great turmoil. He was convinced that God was against him. When I asked why he had come to that conclusion, he rattled off a whole litany of things; his wife temporarily leaving him, his children's rebellion and disobedience, his continuing health problems, attendance problems at his church, financial disasters, and the list went on and on. When I asked him if he believed that God really loved him he said on one hand he did. After all, God sent His precious Son to die on his behalf. On the other hand, almost everything in his life seemed to indicate that God had it out for him. The bottom line was a serious lack of inner peace because He was so conflicted in his feelings about God.

I asked him if he ever heard inner voices telling him that "God doesn't care about you," or "God is punishing you," or "God really doesn't love you." He looked at me kind of surprised and said, "Yes." He figured that was just self-talk responding to the flesh and to his difficult life situations. I told him that I believed Satan was doing a number on him and that he needed to put on the "sandals of peace."

When Paul talks about "having shod your feet with the preparation of the gospel of peace,"[39] he was, again, not speaking of becoming a Christian. The Ephesian believers were already Christians. He was encouraging them to put something on that would give them spiritual stability or grip; that is what the word "preparation" actually means. What gives a Christian spiritual stability is believing the "gospel of peace"; that is, believing that through the death and resurrection of Jesus Christ we have peace with God.[40] It is believing that although before Christ we were enemies of God,[41] now we are in a peaceful relationship with God, and He is for us and not in any way against us.[42] When we grasp this truth it is like putting on the sandals that Roman Legionnaires wore in battle.[43] These were not the flimsy, thinly soled sandals with laces that went up the legs. No, these were very sturdy sandals with soles almost an inch thick with hobnails embedded in them. These nails protruded out of the bottom of the sandals so they looked a lot like modern football or soccer cleats. When the Roman soldier was fighting in mud or slippery grass he had to be able to stand his ground. He had to know that his feet would not slip while thrusting his sword against the enemy. His sandals ensured solid grip in almost any kind of terrain or weather conditions.

We need the same kind of spiritual grip because Satan and his forces are regularly trying to convince us that there is a problem between us and God. That's what happened with Job. Remember his situation? Satan challenged the wisdom and truthfulness of God's plan to create men and women who would voluntarily love and serve Him.[44] Job unfortunately became Exhibit A. Satan was allowed to take away almost everything from Job except his life. I also believe that Satan was indirectly speaking through Job's wife when she said to Job: "Curse God, and die!"[45] When God allows us to suffer for His glory and our spiritual growth, Satan's message is "God is against you" or "God isn't fair to you." The devil tries to get us to believe that even though Christ died for us in the greatest act of love ever, God still has a problem with us and doesn't really care about us.

Now it is true that God sometimes tests us as believers to confirm our righteousness (like Job), or to bring us to maturity in Christ.[46] These times of testing can be quite difficult. It can give us the impression that God doesn't really care about us like He once did. So we need to realize what God is doing, trust that He loves us with an everlasting love because of Christ,[47] and resist Satan's attempts to cause a rift between us and our God. I realize this is easy to say and hard to do, but we must fight this battle with the Lord's help and win. Our peace of mind and our harmonious fellowship with God depends on it.

Another related issue is God's discipline of His children. The Bible tells us that when we belong to God through Christ, He will at times severely discipline us because He loves us. Sometimes the discipline is so severe it is like being scourged.[48] The writer of Hebrews tell us that God's discipline is a strong indicator that we truly belong to Him,[49] and that even though God's correction is very unpleasant, it is for our ultimate "good."[50] Satan, of course, tries to convince us that God has turned on us or never really cared about us in the first place. He will tell us that God is still angry with us and is punishing us for our sins.

Now this is a very important point that many Christians today do not fully understand. The Holy Spirit is grieved by our sin,[51] but God is no longer angry with us, even when we sin, because Christ's death satisfied the righteousness of God.[52] The Holy Spirit is disappointed with us when we sin, and since He lives within us, we may feel that disappointment in profound ways. But there is not one New Testament verse that indicates that God is in any way angry with believers, and that means He never punishes us. Punishment is given to satisfy the anger of the one offended and to bring justice to the offended party. When Christ died on the cross He addressed both of those issues. He took our punishment, and God's anger over sin was poured out on Him, so Paul can say, "There is therefore now no condemnation for those who are in Christ Jesus."[53]

Satan cannot have us once we are safely in the hands of the Father through trust in Christ, so he tries for the next best thing from his perspective, that is, to cause a huge rift in our relationship with God. If he can convince us that God doesn't truly care about us or that God is really angry and offended with us, he can succeed in driving a wedge between us and God.

I think of a young man who had a good job, a beautiful wife, two great kids, a nice house, a leadership position in a growing church...he had it all! Then one day his young wife had a stroke, and his entire world collapsed around him. He was so confused. What had he done to offend God? He could think of nothing. Why was God so angry with him? There was no apparent reason. The whole thing seemed so incredibly unfair to him. Of course, Satan was encouraging this young believer to assume the worst, and for a while, he did. Then, without warning, while he was just playing with his kids in the driveway, he was overwhelmed by the love of God. The Holy Spirit simply impressed upon him that God loved him with a great everlasting love.[54] He realized that nothing that had happened to him was because God was angry or indifferent toward him. God had a plan for him and his family that was good and loving, and he simply needed to trust God and rest in His love. That day Satan was defeated, but it took direct intervention on God's part to bring this man back to his spiritual senses. God will do this for us at times,[55] but He has commanded us to keep this from happening by putting on the sandals of peace. When we understand and affirm that "through Jesus Christ I now have peace with God, and God is for me and not in any way against me," we have put on the sandals of peace. We need this spiritual armor on every day of our lives because whenever something apparently goes wrong in our lives, Satan is going to tell us "God's out to get you." That is why we must have the sandals of peace on our spiritual feet. However, even this is not sufficient to protect us. Don't forget about the shield of faith.

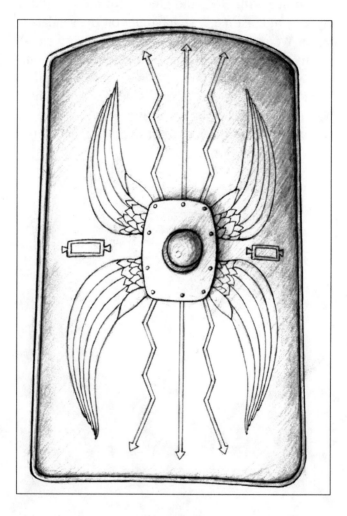

The Shield of Faith

Chapter 5

The Shield of Faith

When I was pastoring a church in Iowa, I was responsible for hundreds of souls in a rather large country church. After several years I knew a little something about, just about everyone. That's the way it is in small towns—no secrets. However, one tall, quiet woman was almost a complete mystery to me. I can't remember hearing anything about her or having her say anything to me that gave me a clue about who she was until one day she showed up at my office. As soon as she was ushered through the door she broke down in tears.

In a barely audible voice she told me how her father and older brothers sexually molested her for several years. From about age seven until she was old enough to finally fight them off, this horrific crime happened on a regular basis. She lived for years in fear and guilt. In fact, the guilt continued on right up until the day that I spoke with her. She told me that she blamed herself for what happened. I asked her why. She said that a voice inside her head kept telling her that she must have encouraged this terrible behavior, or it would not have continued for years. I empathetically told her that the "voice" she was hearing was either her unrenewed mind or, more likely, a demon, and I told her in no uncertain terms that she was not responsible for the sexual abuse she had endured for so long. I encouraged her to stop and pray out loud for God to help her believe that she was not to blame and to ask Him to keep Satan away from her. She prayed a beautiful prayer, but when she finished she looked at me funny and said, "I just heard a voice say – 'you're still to blame, and you still belong to me.'" Now I knew for sure who we were dealing with. I explained how Satan throws his fiery darts of accusation and deception into our minds. I assured her that if she was trusting Christ as her Savior, she belonged to God, and I encouraged her to use the shield of faith to defend herself against Satan. That day that precious soul achieved a lasting victory over Satan. Unfortunately, many, many Christians have accusing or deceptive thoughts and figure it is either the Holy Spirit convicting them, or it is just self-talk that may or may not be correct. This is why we need the shield of faith.

The Bible tells us that Satan shoots his fiery darts at us.[56] Somehow he launches his accusations and lies into our minds so that we think these awful missiles are either the voice of the spirit or our own human thoughts. The shield of faith is what enables us to combat these attacks and discern their origin.

To understand the shield of faith and how we need to deploy it, we must go back to the Roman legionnaire. The legionnaire would be supplied with a very large rectangular shield that was almost as tall as he was. It was designed to protect his entire body from spears and arrows. The shield was curved to deflect blows from swords and cause incoming arrows and spears to glance off. But the shield was also designed to protect the soldier when there was a direct hit. The outer frame of this shield was covered by layers of fabric and leather. Before the soldier would go out to battle, he would thoroughly soak the shield in water so that when fiery arrows pierced the shield, they would be extinguished without causing further damage or harm. The defensive strategy was taken a step further when the soldiers were ordered to form a "turtle" or "tortoise."

The turtle formation was ordered when Romans soldiers were attacking a fortress or would be coming under attack by arrows and spears. Many soldiers would come together: those in the middle would hold their shields over their head, and the soldiers on the outside of the rectangular formation would carry their shield in front, behind, or to their right or left side with their long spears coming out next to their shield. This mobile formation was the forerunner of modern armored tanks. It also resembled a turtle with spikes coming out of it—thence the name.

The Turtle

In relation to spiritual warfare, all this background is very important. We are to deploy the shield of faith in a similar manner. We must hold the shield of faith up to protect ourselves, especially for our heads, as Satan fires his accusing and deceptive messages into our minds. As mentioned before, sometimes Satan uses a demon to whisper in our ear, but often Satan is simply using the world's messages to bombard us each day.

I once read that in the course of any given day our minds are assaulted with literally thousands of messages through peers, the media, teachers, signs, etc. Satan uses these to try and influence us and conform us to the world's way of thinking and acting. This is why Paul says, "do not be conformed to this world, but be transformed by the renewing of your mind..."[57] Exactly how do we renew our minds? How does all this relate to the shield of faith? For the answer we must look at what the apostle Paul says in II Corinthians 10:3-5: "For though we walk in the flesh, we do not war according to the flesh, for the weapons of our warfare are not of the flesh, but divinely powerful for the destruction of fortresses. We are destroying speculations and every lofty thing raised up against the knowledge of God, and we are taking every thought captive to the obedience of Christ..."

Renewing of one's mind begins with the shield of faith "...taking every thought captive to the obedience of Christ...." This means that as we go through our day with the shield of faith protecting our mind, we are not just letting messages, voices, and thoughts pass through our minds unexamined or worse, letting those thoughts dwell in our minds. Rather, every message, voice, and thought is being held captive as it comes in, and we compare it to the truth of God's Word. If it does not meet the criteria of Philippians 4:8, we reject it and with God's help, banish it from our thinking. We should only allow those thoughts which are true, honorable, right, pure, lovely and of good report to remain in our minds. This is the basic process of renewing one's mind utilizing the shield of faith, but Paul warns us about two particular types of satanic lies that we need to destroy when Satan sends them our way. The first is "speculations."

This term seems at a glance to refer to something that is relatively harmless. What could be so bad about speculations? This word from the Greek word we translate *logistics*. It refers to concepts that sound quite logical, but are, in fact, very wrong. A good example is what I hear from time to time about loving oneself. People say, "I have to love myself before I can love others." This sounds extremely logical and right, and there is a sense in which it is true. We need to see ourselves as we are in Christ which leads to a healthy self-respect, but self-love is a different matter. When we focus on loving ourselves we never have the time and energy for loving others. We are a bottomless pit of need. If we focus on ourselves we will never be satisfied. When we focus on loving others, they benefit, and we are blessed as well. Satan is constantly trying to shoot speculations into our thinking to ruin our lives and relationships. We must use the shield of faith to trap and then extinguish them.

Another specific fiery arrow that needs to be destroyed is "lofty things." Again, this may sound pretty innocent, but this term refers to thoughts or ideas that sound really profound but are actually nonsense. A British atheist and evolutionist named Huxley used to say, "evolution is impossible, but it happened." If something is impossible, it cannot naturally happen, and if it does happen, it is by definition a miracle, an act of God. An evolutionist saying that evolution is a miracle, but God had nothing to do with it, is both bad science and bad religion. Many people, even some Christians, readily accept such statements today as great wisdom. This is yet another reason why we must take every thought captive with the shield of faith— rejecting the wrong and accepting only what is "good and acceptable and perfect."[58]

What about when a person has already allowed satanic lies and accusations to dwell in his or her mind? What about when a person has already accepted these satanic lies and deceptions and they are deeply ingrained in their thinking? This is what the Bible refers to as "fortresses" and more specifically, "strongholds."[59] Strongholds were mighty towers that were built both in and outside of ancient cities. They were very difficult to attack and overcome. They were not easily overthrown. When people have bought into satanic lies and accusations for years, it is hard to destroy them. They are spiritual and emotional strongholds.

I'll never forget hearing Morgan Fairchild, one of television's most beautiful women, say that when she looks in the mirror she still sees a fat, little girl. How could that be possible? She hasn't been a fat, little girl for ages, if ever. Satan at some point convinced her that she was a fat, unattractive person, and she believed it, and it has become a stronghold for her. She is not alone. Many Christians have also accepted satanic lies and accusations that are now strongholds for them. These strongholds usually require counseling and discipleship to tear them down. It is sometimes a difficult and painful process, but if a Christian is willing to face the truth, God can help them to begin destroying these strongholds that sap our joy and hinder our growth. Once the strongholds are destroyed, we must regularly use the shield of faith to keep new ones from forming in our lives.

But once again, even wielding the shield of faith will not be sufficient to completely protect ourselves from Satan's attacks. We still require the helmet of salvation.

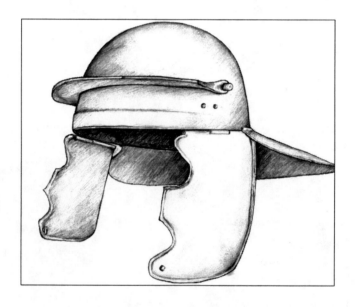

The Helmet of Salvation

Chapter 6

The Helmet of Salvation

Chances are you have seen the *Star Wars* movie entitled, *The Return of the Jedi*. Millions saw it in the theatre, and millions have viewed it on video or DVD. If you haven't seen it or even if you have many times, let me describe what happens when Luke Skywalker confronts his father, Darth Vader.

Luke Skywalker is a Jedi knight who, many years in the future, is fighting for those involved in the rebellion. These are the good guys who are rebelling against the Emperor and all the bad guys of the evil empire. Darth Vader was a good guy, a Jedi knight like Luke, but was convinced to come over to the "dark side" by the Emperor. When it turns out to the surprise of both that his son is Luke Skywalker, attempts are made by both parties to have the other defect to the opposing side. Besides the political issue involved, there is also a spiritual one. The worldview of this movie is that the universe is governed by an impersonal, but all pervasive "force" that has both an evil and a good aspect to it. Luke is on the good side of the force and Darth Vader is on the evil side. In earlier episodes, Luke had struggled with the possibility he might be drawn to the dark side, but after maturing and training by Jedi Master, Yoda, Luke is supremely confident that he can face his father— perhaps even persuade his father to come back to the good side of the Force. In the end, Luke is defeated by Darth Vader in combat, but refuses to turn to the dark side. The Emperor steps in and attempts to kill Luke, but dad, Darth Vader, finally comes around to rescue Luke and destroy the Emperor.

Now I don't agree with the spiritual scenario of the Force. There is only one true and living God who is a person, and He does not have an evil side.[60] Having clearly said that, the spiritual lesson is that Luke was confident enough to confront his father in battle because he believed that there was no way he would be tempted, forced or persuaded to go over to the other side. He knew, win or lose, his destiny was to stay with the good guys. The same principle is important in the true spiritual realm we live in each day.

Many Christians avoid or run away from confrontations with Satan because they are afraid that he could turn their heart away from God, but God has called us to "resist" and "stand firm"[61] which requires us to take a stand. God has promised if we do this in His strength, the devil "will flee"[62] from us. If we are afraid that we will lose our salvation or be tempted to go over to Satan's side, then we will continue to go AWOL (absent without leave). In order to be effective against Satan's attacks and to have peace of mind in the midst of his onslaughts, we must have the confidence that we will not be forced or tempted to switch sides. This is why we need the "helmet of salvation."

In Ephesians 6:17, Paul tells us as Christians to "take the helmet of salvation," but Paul is not encouraging the Ephesians to become believers in Jesus Christ because they have already taken that step of faith. The verb *take* refers to regular, habitual action.[63] We as believers are to regularly put on the helmet of salvation, but if this is not a reference to becoming a Christian by faith in Christ, then what is the helmet of salvation all about? The answer is found, I believe, in I Thessalonians 5:8, the only other place in Scripture where Paul speaks about the helmet of salvation. In this particular verse he refers to it as the "helmet, the hope of salvation." The word *hope* is the key to understanding exactly what the helmet means for us. The word *hope* today sometimes has the connotation of wishful thinking. People will say, "I hope ____ ____ happens," knowing without much doubt it is highly unlikely. In other words, I wish it to happen, but I am almost sure it will not. The word *hope* in Scripture has almost the exact opposite meaning; it indicates a confident expectation[64] that what we wish for will definitely come to pass.

The other help in understanding the helmet of salvation comes from visualizing the helmet worn by the Roman Legionnaire.[65] The combat helmet of this soldier was made of bronze. It was a very heavy helmet designed with check flaps to protect the face, a thick ridge over the brow and crown of the head to deflect blows from a sword, and a graceful extension from the base of the helmet that protruded to protect the back of the neck. When a Roman soldier put this helmet on, he could be confident that his head would be protected against just about any kind of weapon or assault. This confidence gave the Roman soldier a tremendous edge in battle.

The same is true in the spiritual realm. When we as believers affirm that our eternal destiny is secure in Christ and that Satan cannot snatch us away from God by force[66] or tempt us away from our Lord,[67] then we will have the confidence we need to do battle with Satan even if we temporarily give in to temptation or sin.

In I Peter 1:5 the Bible says we are "...protected by the power of God through faith for a salvation ready to be revealed in the last time." Now granted, this verse indicates that we must continue to believe in Jesus Christ, but it also indicates we will because we are protected by the power of God. Ultimately, it is not what we do that keeps us eternally secure, but rather what God does. As Paul says, "faithful is He who calls you, and He will also bring it to pass."[68]

A powerful example of this truth is found in the book, *A Severe Mercy*. It is about a young man named Sheldon Vanauken who was befriended by C.S. Lewis and became a believer in Jesus Christ. He and his wife, Davy, were very much in love. Unfortunately, she died tragically from a terrible disease. As a result, Vanauken struggled with severe doubts about the goodness of God. Satan obviously encouraged those doubts. At a certain point, Vanauken was strongly tempted to abandon his belief in God. He wrote about the conflict.

"I was overwhelmed with a sense of cosmos empty of God as well as Davy. 'All right,' I muttered to myself. 'To hell with God. I'm not going to believe this damned rubbish anymore. Lies, all lies. I've been had.' Up I sprang and rushed out to the country. This was the end of God. Ha!

And then I found I *could not* reject God. I could not. I cannot explain this. One discovers one cannot move a boulder by trying with all one's strength to do it. I discovered—without any sudden influx of love or faith—that I could not reject Christianity. Why I don't know. There it was. I could not.[69]

I know why Vanauken could not go over to the other side. He, like every believer in Jesus Christ, is protected by the power of God, and that is why we should not be afraid of Satan. He may temporarily harm us by tempting us to sin, but he cannot eternally hurt us. He will encourage us to doubt, but ultimately we will keep believing because of the power of God. As John says, "...greater is He who is in you than he who is in the world."[70]

To put on the helmet of salvation we simply affirm that *I can resist Satan with the confidence that my salvation is secure in Christ. Satan cannot tempt me away or snatch me away from God.* When we say this and believe it, we will have the ability to do battle with Satan, knowing that even if we lose a particular battle, we will still win the war. I need that

confidence and so do you. However, even with all the
pieces of armor that we have discussed, we still need
one more. The only offensive weapon we have been
given is the "sword of the Spirit."

The Sword of the Spirit

Chapter 7

The Sword of the Spirit

⸷

I had the privilege years ago of leading a Vietnam veteran to saving faith in Jesus Christ. He was and is a man's man and he actually experienced combat in the Vietnam War. A lot of American soldiers never did. He was a platoon leader and fought against both the North Vietnamese regulars, who he said were very tough, professional fighters, and the V.C. or Viet Cong, who he considered to be more of a nuisance than real soldiers. I asked him what was the toughest lesson new soldiers had to learn. He replied that one could always tell the guys who had been "in country" for a while from the new drafters or recruits. The dead giveaway was how much ammunition they took when going out on a patrol or mission. The new soldiers took lots of food, clothing, and equipment. The guys who had actually been in combat a few times took all the ammunition they could possibly carry. They knew from experience that one could live without a lot of things, but in an intense fire fight, when it was a life and death situation, a soldier needs all the ammunition he can lay his hands on. The same principle is true in our spiritual battles. When Satan attacks us, we need all the ammo we can get, and just like the soldiers in Vietnam, we have to pack it with us before we get into a combat situation. Otherwise, it's too late.

As said before, we have been given only one offensive weapon by God: it is the "sword of the Spirit." Paul says it is "the word of God." So, our only offensive weapon is God's word, the Bible. Now, this does not mean we go looking for trouble. Our position is a defensive one, yet we need to be able to defend ourselves when Satan or any of his demonic forces attack.

It is interesting to note that the Roman legion-naire did not carry the long sword used in dress ceremonies or by the calvary soldiers.[71] Rather, these foot soldiers utilized a much shorter double-edged sword also favored by Roman gladiators. This sword was much quicker to draw and easier to wield. It was not swung about like we sometimes see in old war movies. It was used to jab and thrust at the enemy during close quarter fighting. It was the perfect sword for hand-to-hand combat.

Back to the spiritual realm, our sword is the Word of God, but it is not long portions of Scripture that we look up in our Bible during the heat of battle. We need short, well-rehearsed and memorized verses that we can quickly speak out to defeat satanic powers. When I say "speak out," I mean out loud because that is what the Scripture indicates. The term *word* of God in Ephesians 6:17 refers not to written words but spoken words. Why? Satan and his demons cannot read your mind. God knows the thoughts and intents of our minds and hearts,[72] but Satan, although he is a formidable foe, is not God. He can sometimes tell what we are thinking by watching our behavior, but when it comes right down to it, he cannot know for sure what we are thinking. We have to speak out loud for him to hear us. If you think I am wrong about this, check out how Jesus dealt with Satan. He spoke God's Word to him out loud. Normally-speaking, we should do the same. Besides, it is important for us to hear what we are thinking. It is encouraging and motivating for us to say, like Jesus, "Be gone Satan."[73] We need to hear ourselves resisting the devil. We need to follow the example of our Lord and learn about Satan's strategies from His experience with the Devil in the wilderness.

When Satan tempted Jesus, he used three basic strategies of temptation. First, he tried to make sin appear reasonable.[74] Jesus had not eaten much for forty days, and He was hungry. The devil said, "If you are the Son of God, command that these stones become bread." This appears to be a perfectly reasonable request. What could be wrong with eating a little after fasting so long? Nothing, until it causes us to value food above God's Word or distracts us from hearing what God is saying which is much more important in life. This is why Jesus quoted Deuteronomy 8:3 which says, "Man shall not live by bread alone, but on every word that proceeds out of the mouth of God." Notice that Satan did not ask Jesus to do something that was obviously and clearly wrong. He encouraged Jesus to do what seemed *reasonable,* but it was, in fact, sinful. We need to be wary of these kinds of temptations. Eating, drinking, having nice houses and cars are not inherently wrong, but if they become more important to us than God's Word, or distract us from hearing God's Word, then we have a problem.

The second way that Satan tempted Christ was by making sin appear *right.*[75] Again, this is not a frontal attack on the truth, but rather a subtle attempt to distort the truth. Satan takes Jesus to the pinnacle of the Temple. This is not the roof of the Temple; it is the edge of the Temple mount. From this location it is well over a hundred feet down to the Kidron Valley to the rocks below. The devil was encouraging Jesus to throw Himself off so His angels could stop His fall and everyone would know He was the Messiah. This all sounds very right, but it is, in fact, very wrong because Jesus says, "you shall not put the Lord your God to the test."[76] We cannot demand that God do anything. Even things He has promised to do. It is not our place to say when, where or how God will fulfill His promises. Our responsibility is to humbly remind God of His Word and then trust Him for the timing and means of fulfillment.

When the subtle approaches fail, Satan will try something more direct.[77] He attempts to make sin appear *beautiful.* He takes our Lord to a high mountain and gives Him a breathtaking, panoramic view of all the wonderful places in this world. Then he offers "all these things" if Jesus will fall down and worship him. Our Lord tells him to "be gone" because "you shall worship the Lord your God, and serve Him only."[78] Satan offered Jesus the kingdom without a cross. He offered Him the prize without any suffering, but our Lord could never do this if it meant giving to Satan what belongs alone to God, and neither should we.

The temptation of Christ shows us that Satan will try to tempt us by making sin look reasonable, wrong appear right, and by showing us the easy, beautiful side of evil. Our responsibility is to be spiritually alert and in prayer throughout the day so that we are not deceived. We are to look out not just for ourselves but for our family and other believers as well.[79] And when we discern that we are being tempted, like Christ, we need to respond with Scripture.

When Satan tells us that we are ugly, worthless or nothing important, we can say, "I am 'His workmanship created in Christ Jesus.'"[80] The term *workmanship* could be translated *masterpiece* because this term can refer to the creation of an artist.[81] In Christ we have real value, worth, and beauty, and we should not let the devil tell us any differently.

When someone says something very wrong or offensive to us and a demon whispers in our ear, "let 'em have it," we need to say, "be angry, but don't sin."[82] That's for us, not for the offending party! Anger can motivate us to do what is right, but it is also one of the primary ways that the devil uses to get us into sin.[83]

When Satan encourages us to love anything or anyone more than God, we must remind him that "... you shall love the Lord your God with all your heart and all your soul and with all your mind."[84]

In short, we need to be well armed with plenty of biblical ammo. We can say as Jesus did, "be gone Satan" in His name. But to truly follow His example, and to be most effective, and to convince ourselves about what we are doing, we should speak God's Word aloud.

Over the last several years I have been involved in ministry in more than one Caribbean country. I have found that while Satan is definitely alive and well in the USA, he is much bolder and open in places where he is regularly worshipped by significant portions of the population. On one occasion I was with a group that was doing street evangelism in an island town. While my oldest son was sharing the gospel, a man wandered up to the group and began acting very strange. His movements were very erratic, and he kept walking in and around them. Then he began to interrupt the gospel presentation. At this moment I realized this man was no ordinary heckler, he was either demon controlled or possessed. In either case I was compelled to address it. I caught his eye and said, "I'm telling you in the name of Jesus to be silent because every knee is going to bow and every tongue is going to confess that He is Lord." I am not even sure that I quoted the most appropriate Scripture, but he immediately became quiet and settled down. A number of people ended up praying to put their trust in Christ, and all was forgotten until later that night when he showed up again. This time we were showing the *Jesus* film and about a hundred people were there to view it. We knew he was there by satanic directive to make a disturbance. Several in our group surrounded him, and one lady in particular confronted him. During questioning he confessed that he had sold his soul to Satan in a demonic ceremony a few years before. He also told us that he felt compelled by this agreement to engage in sexual and degrading practices that he hated and that more than anything he wished he could be free of. He said, with tears in his eyes, "I can never be free again. I am in bondage." We quickly told him that if he would put his trust in Jesus, the Lord would deliver him and set him free forever.[85] He looked at us like we were crazy, but after some pleading and insisting that Jesus really could help him, he finally prayed and asked Jesus to be his Savior. At that point, he felt a great burden lifted and instead of tears of agony, there were tears of joy! We instructed him about how to resist Satan by using, among other weapons, the sword of the Spirit. We encouraged him to tell Satan, whenever he tried to reclaim his prize, that "in Christ, he is a new creation, old things have passed away..."[86]

About a year later I saw his pastor and asked about how he was doing. His pastor told me with a big smile that our friend had destroyed all his idols, was no longer involved in any sexual immorality, and was growing in the grace and knowledge of the Lord Jesus Christ!

Armed with the sword of the Spirit we can resist Satan and have the victory over demonic forces, but we cannot rely exclusively on just one or two, or even three or four of our spiritual weapons. We need all six pieces of armor, and we must be able to put them on quickly. Can we? Absolutely and I will tell you how.

The Legionnaire

Conclusion

Putting on the Armor in One Minute

On May 28, 1977, at the Beverly Hills Supper Club in Southgate, Kentucky, an estimated 2,500 people were eating and enjoying the club's entertainment with no idea of what was about to happen. At about ten minutes to nine a fire broke out in one of the many reception rooms and quickly spread. A busboy named Walter Bailey interrupted the act in the Cabaret Room and announced that there was a small fire. Some of the people gathered just laughed, thinking it was a comedy routine. Some brushed it off and continued eating and drinking because it was just a "small fire." Within minutes the entire building was in flames, and one hundred and sixty-five people did not escape.

I trust that you realize at this point that you and your loved ones are in real spiritual danger. I hope that no one is writing off the warning of this book.

There have been many spiritual casualties over the years, and that is such a tragedy because, although the spiritual danger is real, immediate and serious, there is no reason you or your loved ones have to be victims. You can put on the full armor of God and be protected against whatever Satan throws at you, and you can do it in about one minute!

Putting on the full armor consists of saying and believing these things:

Belt of Truth	I will know and act on what God says is true, regardless of how I feel at any particular moment.
Breastplate of Righteousness	I am a saint who is righteous in Jesus Christ. I don't have to sin and Satan cannot make me.
Sandals of Peace	I have peace with God through the Lord Jesus Christ. Therefore, God is for me and is not against me in any way.
Shield of Faith	I will capture every thought that comes into my mind, accepting only what is true and rejecting whatever is false.
Helmet of Salvation	I can resist Satan with the confidence that my salvation is secure in Christ. Satan cannot tempt me away or snatch me away from God.

Sword of the Spirit   I will speak the Word of God to resist Satan whenever he tries to tempt me or attack me.

These six pieces of spiritual armor can be memorized and then recited whenever needed (this is what I personally recommend), or this spiritual armor can be put on a card to be pulled out and spoken aloud when necessary. In either case, the armor of God can be put on in about one minute which is very important because Satan can strike very quickly. This may take a little practice and some effort, but it is worth it. I cannot urge you strongly enough to take this step of faith every day and as often as needed.

Now you may say that your situation is really, really bad. Let me conclude with a true story that I hope convinces you that no matter how difficult or desperate your situation, you can have victory through our Lord Jesus Christ.

I know a beautiful family that was on the brink of being torn apart. The husband and wife had been believers in Jesus Christ for many years and appeared to be model Christians. Both were very involved in their church and were actively serving the Lord in a number of ways. In reality, he was so involved at church and in his own recreation that he had little time for her, and she greatly resented it. She, because of childhood issues and her husband's neglect, turned to other men and was involved in multiple affairs, one going on for years. At a certain point, it appeared their marriage was doomed, and the children were fearful and insecure. At this critical point, both became aware of Satan's involvement in their situation. Without excusing their own responsibility for their plight, the couple realized that Satan was behind the scenes actively working to destroy their marriage, their family, their Christian testimony and everything else that was worthwhile in life. By putting on the armor of God and committing to change their behavior for the Lord and each other, this couple snatched victory from the jaws of defeat. He determined to forgive and love her as he ought. She made a decision to seek counseling and learn more about how God sees us in Christ. The bottom line is that this family is together today and growing in Christ because they recognized they were under spiritual attack, and they took the necessary steps to gain the victory. They did with God's help, and so can you!

Whatever your personal situation, no matter how long you have been defeated or how grim things may appear, victory through the Lord Jesus Christ is attainable. You have to recognize Satan's role, take personal responsibility for your actions and attitudes, and put on the whole armor of God. You can do it in about one minute. Why not now?

"Thanks be to God who gives us the victory through our Lord Jesus Christ."
I Corinthians 15:57

Endnotes

[1]*The Battle Is the Lord's*, Tony Evans, Moody Press, p. 201

[2]Dennis Dehaan, *Windows on the Word*, Baker, p. 12

[3]II Timothy 2:3

[4]Ephesians 1:18-19

[5]Ephesians 1:20

[6]Ephesians 1:21-22

[7]Ephesians 2:6

[8]Ephesians 6:10

[9]See *Spiritual Warfare* by Richard Ing as an example of a book that espouses exorcism or "deliverance" as the most important aspect of spiritual warfare.

[10]Matthew 10:1

[11]Acts 16:16-18

[12]See *Spiritual Warfare for Every Christian* by Dean Sherman, YWAM, p. 195.

[13]Matthew 12:29

[14]Colossians 2:15

[15]Jude 9

[16]Ephesians 6:13, I Peter 5:9, and James 4:7

[17]Evans, p. 201

[18]Ephesians 6

[19]Ephesians 6:12

[20]See also Colossians 1:16 for another list of demonic ranks.

[21]*Demon Possession and the Christian*, Fred Dickason, Moody Press, p. 200

[22]II Corinthians 10:4

[23]Ephesians 6:14

[24]Genesis 3:1

[25]Genesis 3:2,3

[26]Genesis 3:4,5

[27]I Corinthians 6:12,13

[28]James 4:1,2

[29]James 1:14

[30]Galatians 5:16

[31]Galatians 3:27

[32]I Corinthians 1:2

[33]I John 1:8

[34]W. Bauer, W.F. Arndt, F.W. Gingrich, U of Chicago Press, p. 102

[35]I John 4:4

[36]As cited in What's So Amazing About Grace?, Yancy, Zondervan, p. 37-38

[37]I John 1:10

[38]Colossians 2:13-15

[39]Ephesians 6:15

[40]Romans 5:1

[41]Romans 5:10

[42]Romans 8:31-34

[43]See illustration on page 42.

[44]Job 1:8-11

[45]Job. 2:9

[46]James 1:2-4
[47]Romans 8:35-39
[48]Hebrews 12:6
[49]Hebrews 12:7-8
[50]Hebrews 12:10-11
[51]Ephesians 4:30
[52]I John 2:2
[53]Romans 8:1
[54]Romans 5:5
[55]See the author's book, Why Christians Sin for a more complete explanation of how God deals with wayward and disillusioned believers.
[56]Ephesians 6:16
[57]Romans 12:2
[58]Romans 12:2
[59]II Corinthians 10:4
[60]James 1:13
[61]Ephesians 6:13
[62]James 4:7
[63]The aorist tense here refers to customary, habitual action
[64]BAGD, p. 252
[65]See illustration on page 60
[66]John 10:28
[67]John 10:27
[68] I Thessalonians 5:24
[69]A Severe Mercy, Sheldon Vanauken, Harper and Row, p. 191.
[70]I John 4:4
[71]See illustration on page 68
[72]Psalm 139:4; I Samuel 16:7
[73]Matthew 4:10

[74]Matthew 4:1-4
[75]Matthew 4:5-7
[76]Deuteronomy 6:16
[77]Matthew 4:8-10
[78]Deuteronomy 6:13
[79]Ephesians 6:18
[80]Ephesians 2:10
[81]BAGD, p. 689.
[82]Ephesians 4:26
[83]Ephesians 4:27
[84]Matthew 22:37
[85]John 8:36
[86]II Corinthians 5:17